Life Map to Mongolia:

Overcoming the Odds

To Heather

from one adventurous woman to another. Love Rose

Rosemary Sales

ISBN: 978-1-0369-3374-6

Printed and bound by:
Print Plus Hereford
126 Widemarsh Street
Hereford
HR4 9HN

To Simon and our wonderful children

About the Author

Rosemary Sales is the Director of the Wye Knot Community, which she founded in 2018. She initially ignited her love of nature through escaping a troubled childhood to her early career as an activities coordinator.

Now Rosemary shares her remarkable skills through her intergenerational work, leading wilderness adventures aimed at women, and inspiring others to learn about wellbeing through shared outdoor experiences.

Close to her heart is her passion for the River Wye, with many hours spent swimming, paddleboarding and exploring in Boudicca, her beloved canoe. This led to the invitation to travel to Mongolia to test her canoeing abilities in one of the most remote parts of the world and gave her a unique opportunity to reflect on her own life experiences in a completely different environment.

Rosemary lives in Herefordshire with her husband Simon, their two teenage children and a small dog called Oz.

Contents

Introduction

They say life's a journey, not a destination. Well, mine has been quite the adventure. From the chaos of my childhood to the heights of personal achievement, I've experienced it all. My life has been a whirlwind of highs and lows. From the joy of motherhood and the thrill of love to the challenges of adversity and the pain of loss, I've weathered every storm and learned to laugh in the face of adversity, to find strength in weakness, and to persevere when all hope seems lost.

Now, I'm ready to share my story. It's a story of resilience, determination, and unwavering belief in oneself. Join me as I delve into the depths of my past, exploring the trials and triumphs that have shaped me into the person I am today – a journey made richer by the love and support of my husband and beloved children. I have experienced unimaginable hardship. I have been abused, tortured, and my voice has been silenced. But this is not the story I choose to tell.

This is me now: I have overcome adversity and found joy in the face of unimaginable pain. As I often remind myself:

"If you let negative experiences ruin your future and use them as an excuse not to be successful, then you have no chance of overcoming trauma. Use it as power. Use it to make up for the time you lost, the love you never had. Find your own family, create your own future! Because the one thing you have is resilience and real-life experience."

Strangely, I believe those experiences, as horrific as they were, have given me a unique perspective on life. I wouldn't trade them for the world, not because I wish to relive them, but because they have shaped me into the person I am today. They have taught me to appreciate the simple joys in life, to cherish every moment, and to find beauty in the unexpected. I try to live in the present, to savour every day. The present is all we truly have, and it's the only moment that truly matters.

"When life gets hard, don't give up – go on an adventure."

Rosemary Sales, Herefordshire, August 2025

Chapter 1: Who am I now?

I'd never been to Mongolia and I don't know anyone that had. The fact is a lot of people I know don't even know where it is. But the idea of it haunted me in the best way. Vast, wild, untamed. It calls to people who've fought to become who they are. When training officially started it was a whole new world at dawn and I was part nerves, part exhilaration, and all heart.

This was more than an expedition. It was a reckoning. A culmination. A powerful declaration to the girl who was never supposed to arrive here. I wasn't born equipped for this. I was born into chaos. I can't read as well as I'd like, and I never finished school. I taught myself everything after I turned 16. I haven't stopped learning since then. I remember going to school and watching my guardians burn or tear up my books. They didn't want me to be educated for control.

I couldn't even spell my name until I was 12. I started smoking as it was easier to get cigarettes than it was food. I could roll a cigarette before I could write my name. That was one of my jobs as 'small hands are good for rolling'. Apparently, I was good at prison rollies, what an achievement!

I could do a lot of things before I learned to read and write. It's funny to think I'm now writing a book. I knew which berries were safe to eat and how to steal food. Those skills were more important to me back then than learning to read. Survival was the top priority. Maybe that's why I enjoy survival activities now. There's something about surviving that makes you stronger. I swear by it. The fight-or-flight response? I've always been a fighter. I don't think I've ever been truly frightened. I'm not scared of polar bears, but that's for another adventure. I want to go to the North or South Pole, or maybe even Siberia. The Arctic Circle is one of my next challenges. We'll see. Maybe it'll be the subject of my next book!

My childhood taught me that survival mattered more than anything else. At 13, I was kept a house prisoner, and not one person noticed – not even the school, which simply put me down as a 'troubled child'. At 16, an abuser threatened to traffic me once I "turned legal" so I ran and never looked back. Years later, that same abuser received an 18-year sentence. The court gave me closure, but I found freedom in every determined step I took away from that life.

In the 20 years since, I've rebuilt from the ashes. I earned my Forest School Leader qualifications and led an award-winning, funded intergenerational forest project, the first of its kind in the UK. That case study still lives on my website and has inspired others to launch their own forest schools. I founded Wye Knot Community, transforming Herefordshire's cross-generational landscape, bringing together toddlers and centenarians through shared learning in nature. My women's empowerment work has reached over 100 women teaching outdoor skills, mindset shifts, and reconnecting them with the natural world.

I've hosted on my own wilderness weekends and led a three-week empowerment expedition across the wilds of Sweden. I've worked with military families via armed forces welfare services, supporting the wives and partners of serving personnel. Over two decades, I've chased qualifications: Movement Therapy for dementia care, British Canoeing certifications in paddle boarding and canoeing, and I even cracked both English and maths, after previously failing maths six times!

NY WEEKLY MAGAZINE

(Image: NY Weekly)

In the previous summer I was named one of the Top 20 Women Leaders to Look Out For in 2024 by *NY Weekly*. This is what they said: 'Rosemary Sales stands as a powerful example of how lived experience, deep compassion, and fearless leadership can spark real community change. Her work spans generations and borders, proving that resilience can be a movement'.

In my twenties, I faced a tumour while my two brothers and partner served in Afghanistan with the Parachute Regiment. Sam was 18 when a blast nearly took him and claimed three of his friends. He was awarded a Mention in Dispatches, but it cost him pieces of himself. He doesn't talk about this.

Unfortunately, he felt let down by those in charge. When another friend tragically died by suicide in the room above him, Sam decided to transfer to the RAF, desperate to forget everything. The RAF truly looked after him, and I can't thank them enough. In fact, they saw his potential, and he's becoming an officer.
And then there's Simon, my husband. The man I married... three times. Once wasn't enough for our kind of love. Simon has walked with diplomats, global scientists and soldiers. He's seen courage in others, yet he says I'm the strongest person he knows. Not because he's my husband, but because he feels it through his bones when he says it. He doesn't toss compliments on the breeze. He pauses, and then he tells me:

"When I look at you, I see the rarest kind of magic and strength".

We stand side by side fierce, soft, whole. Our love is the kind people think only exists in novels. But it's ours. It is wild. It is real. The scars and the triumphs, they've formed me. I failed. I fell. I got up. Hundreds of times. I built from nothing. I earned every qualification, every title, every moment of peace.

And when motherhood arrived it was with no instruction manual: no familial blueprint to follow. I trusted my instincts. Before Google, before parenting podcasts, I turned to the earth, to nature's rhythms. My children and I became a wolfpack: tight, resilient, unbreakable. They came first. Always. And they still matter most to me every single day.

Going back to my school days...Those memories can be intense, but for now, let's turn our attention to my training. Today, I'm doing some strength training to tone my glutes. Yes, my buns! I need strong legs to carry heavy loads. I want to be strong, ready, and professional. Plus, I want to prevent injuries. Preparation is key to successful trips. I don't want to get injured, so I train a lot. It's important to keep your body, mind, and soul ready for anything. If someone told me right now: 'You're going to walk 40 kilometres with nothing but a knife', I think I'd be ready. I want to be prepared for any challenge. We all should be. It's the way you go about it!

We overthink things sometimes. Let's look at our prehistoric ancestors before *Homo sapiens.* They did everything we could do. They were our ancestors, incredibly adaptable. They thrived everywhere from icy tundra to warm savannahs, crafting complex tools and even developing sophisticated language. Our ancestors were the original survival experts, and I believe we can tap into those same innate skills, reclaiming the knowledge we need. Let's tap into their skills and regain the knowledge we have in us. We've just got a little lost in a world obsessed with war and money. It's time to rediscover our connection to the Earth and real values.

Chapter 2: A new dawn

Well, it's now the New Year, 2025, a year of fresh starts and new beginnings. After the festive cheer of Christmas subsided, I always found myself pondering the year ahead. This year, I couldn't help but delve into the predictions of Nostradamus. His cryptic quatrains, penned in the 16th century, have fascinated people for centuries with their supposed ability to foresee future events. Though his predictions are often debated and open to interpretation, the very idea of someone from his era attempting to glimpse the future captivated me. It made me wonder if I could predict the future. If I could, I would undoubtedly predict that 2025 would be a year of profound challenges.

Climate change is an undeniable reality, and its impact will continue to intensify. While the Earth itself is incredibly resilient, humanity's future remains uncertain. We often forget that the Earth has existed for billions of years, long before our arrival. We take it for granted, this magnificent planet that sustains us.

We are, after all, made of stardust, as Carl Sagan eloquently put it: "The nitrogen in our DNA, the calcium in our teeth, the iron in our blood, the carbon in our apple pies were made in the interiors of collapsing stars. We are made of starstuff."

I believe everyone should take a moment at New Year to reflect on our relationship with the Earth. Observe the changing seasons, the intricate dance of life unfolding around us. Even in the face of immense challenges, life persists. We are fortunate to experience this incredible gift. Life is a precious gift. That's why I'm determined to live it to the fullest. I'm exploring the world, both inner and outer. I feel a deep connection to nature, a primal yearning that draws me outdoors. When I'm inside, I feel a disconnect, a sense of something missing. Being outdoors, and connecting with the Earth, rejuvenates me. It feels as if I'm drawing sustenance from the very ground beneath my feet.

This interconnectedness, this intricate web of life, is often overlooked. I believe that when we truly connect with the Earth, we unlock a profound sense of peace and inner strength. I wish I could share this feeling with everyone. I encourage everyone to step outside, to feel the Earth beneath their feet, to witness the beauty of the natural world. They will be amazed at how healing and rejuvenating it can be.

It's fascinating to consider the parallels between the Earth's structure and the human body. Just as the Earth has layers - the crust, the mantle, the core - our bodies possess intricate layers too. We have our skin, our muscles, our bones, and our vital organs, all working in harmony to sustain life. Like the Earth, we are composed of the same elements, born from the stars.

(Image: Sarah)

We are, in essence, an expression of the Earth itself. This profound connection often goes unrecognised. We treat the Earth as a separate entity, a resource to be exploited rather than a living being to be honoured and respected. We need to remember that we are an integral part of this intricate web of life. We need to treat the Earth with the same care and compassion that we would show to another human being. We need to nurture it, protect it, and strive to live in harmony with it. Only then can we truly thrive as a species.

This is the link we are missing - the understanding that our well-being is inextricably linked to the well-being of the planet. It's time to reconnect, remember our place within this magnificent ecosystem, and work together to ensure a sustainable future for all.

Over the holidays, I covered over 200 miles on my own two feet. Not just training for Mongolia, but because it's ingrained in my lifestyle. I believe in a balanced life, which for me includes exploring the world on foot. I love to spend days walking, discovering hidden gems in the most unexpected places. For example, I recently visited London and Cardiff, the two capitals of my region, and spent both days walking, seeking out the quietest spaces amidst the bustling crowds.

I always have a 'rain check' on capitals, as I call it. I disconnect from the digital world, the constant barrage of news, and any negativity that may be swirling around. I focus on connecting with nature and the present moment. This helps me maintain my inner peace and find strength within myself.

I've dedicated my life to helping others reconnect with nature and find their inner strength. I work with people from all walks of life, including those living with dementia, children, and women seeking to unleash their inner wild. I believe in empowering individuals to connect with the Earth and cultivate a deeper sense of self. People often assume I've had a privileged upbringing, and that I've always had a comfortable life. Nothing could be further from the truth. My childhood was far from perfect.

Chapter 3: It's a no from me

February 2025. Lately, I've been in a bit of a hole. What was meant to be time off for writing turned into time off for... well, just trying to feel better. I've thrown myself into hiking, cold-water dips, long walks, breath work anything to feel a shift. Normally, nature works like a charm, but this time? Nothing. It's like the spark's been dimmed. Maybe it's the lack of sunshine. Maybe it's the background noise of other people's negativity slowly dragging me down. Maybe it's both.

Let's start with the search and rescue team training. I signed up because I like to do something voluntary every year something that makes a difference. I value my time, especially the skills I've grafted hard to gain. But one thing you can't buy is confidence. People think I'm confident, but underneath, there's always this whisper: You're not good enough. I've always had to try harder. I don't talk about that. I should. I know there's help. But I stayed quiet, pushed through, and passed my assessment. I made it onto the team.

Thing is, I feel uncomfortable. I want to help. I do. But I don't know these people. And I'm not sure how I feel being around them. Sure, they've all got clear Disclosure and Barring Service (DBS) checks, but they're mostly men. And they're the kind of men I usually avoid. I guess this is something I need to work on. I'll keep you posted.

I think being part of a team stirred up old memories. That feeling of being the outsider the kid who didn't fit in. I didn't have the right clothes, I smelt, I even had no hair at one point. One of my abusers shaved it all off. No one asked me if I was okay. Not even the teacher. The kids all just laughed, I was in Year Five. It didn't bother me much back then. I was used to it. But now? I've got feelings. I've got kids of my own. And I think about it and feel this sadness I never used to let in. Someone did that to a little girl. And the world just turned away.

Yes, I know others have it worse. And I am safe now. I've made a good life for myself. I'm a middle-class white woman with a warm home and a loving family. But it doesn't erase the past. It doesn't stop that old ache from creeping in when I'm in a room full of strangers, wondering if I belong. I still say awkward things. I still get dismissed. And part of me lets them dismiss me. I make myself small. I act a bit dizzy, so people will leave me alone. It's a survival trick. A clever one.

So if you know me and I'm not dizzy around you just know that means I trust you. I respect you. I've let my guard down. Writing this is helping. I've been blocked for months. But now the words are flowing again, and it feels like something is shifting.

Another hit came recently with an organisation that works with women. It's a great initiative, founded by military wives, encouraging women to get outside and push themselves. I've been involved before. But this time... it felt I was pushed out because I don't fit in their clique. I applied for their mountaineering training, I offered my time, my experience leading hikes, my work empowering women, and still, it was a no. Then I did one trip, but it felt like I wasn't good enough. Again.

That phrase? It hits like a punch in the chest. Not good enough. I need to be mentally strong for Mongolia. That's the mission now. The light on the horizon. I can't talk to people about this stuff, not properly. I stumble over my words and say the wrong things, because I'm so uncomfortable in my skin sometimes. And people who haven't lived through trauma don't get it. It's good that they haven't, I wouldn't wish trauma on anyone, but sometimes they look down on you.

Like they're better, that look of sympathy it's just pity and I never want that! In fact I pity anyone that will put pity on anyone! Pity is for animals. It's easier to keep my past locked away. To tell no one. But the truth is, I care. I care so deeply. I want to feel good. I want to feel like I belong. I've fought so hard to get here. And right now, I feel like nothing is helping. Not the mountains. Not the sea. Not my incredible children, or even my wonderful husband.

But Mongolia, that's my hope. That's where I'll find my spark again. That's where I'll remember how far I've come. Because right now? Right now, I need to believe that I'm not just 'good enough' – I'm more than enough.

Then all of a sudden I've just figured it out and it's now March 2025. This is why I've been feeling so low lately. It's that time of year again, that strange space where there's no real adventure in my life. Not the kind that challenges me. Not the kind that makes my heart race or demands more of me than I think I've got. I need that hit. That adrenaline to live, that fire, that edge-of-fear feeling. I need the river!

It might sound strange, but if you've been through trauma, if you've lived through abuse or felt true fear then maybe you'll understand. When you spend your early years scared every single day, hyper-aware, walking on eggshells, constantly braced for the world. your body adjusts. That fear becomes familiar. Normal, even. I lived like that for the first 16 years of my life. Until I found the strength to break away. But that fear? It left an imprint.

And now? My life is safe. So safe. I've built a world where nothing can hurt me, where I'm in control. I couldn't be more secure, and somehow, that's the problem.

Because safety makes me feel numb. I can't feel things I normally feel; it's a really strange feeling. It's like I can't get that buzz when I see something truly beautiful. I see it every day, and it just looks the same. I want it to look amazing. I want it to make me think, *I'm alive.* I want to see things and feel them. I don't want to feel numb, and I think maybe safety makes me numb. Strange, isn't it? Maybe I need to work on that, because isn't it normal to feel safe? I'm not sure.

Now, with Mongolia on the horizon, the nerves and excitement are kicking in. The butterflies, the anticipation, the uncertainty. And for the first time in a while I feel alive again. Alive. Like I'm stepping out of the numbness and into the wild.

To live, you have to accept death. You have to know that one day, it's going to happen and that it's completely out of your control. So instead, I'm trading the feeling of safety for something else: power. Choice. I choose the fear now. I choose how much, how far, how wild. No one else. And if you've been through something similar, if trauma has lived in your body, I think you'll understand. This is why I push myself. This is why I adventure. To reclaim what was taken from me. And I'll never let anyone take it again.

(Image: Simon)

I've also been thinking a lot lately. Reflecting, training, preparing. I've been out on the river every free day I've had, putting in the miles in my canoe. Her name is Boudicca, after the Warrior Queen. Her story of rising up against the Roman Empire after unimaginable betrayal, fighting back fiercely and fearlessly, makes her the perfect namesake. She's a powerful symbol of the strength that lives in every woman, especially those who've been told they're powerless – those who have finally had enough.

When I'm paddling, and my blade slices into the water, I feel something deep. Like I'm connecting. Tiny little me in this big, powerful boat in control. I feel strong. I feel free. When I was younger, I used to dream about this being on the river, in a boat, gliding over the water. Anything fun. Anything that felt like an escape. And now, I'm living that dream. Fully. And it's brought me here, to this chapter of my life and I'm the owner of a boat my own boat!

Chapter 4: Fault lines and freedom

I'm about to leave for the trip of a lifetime. It's May 2025. It's exciting. Exhilarating. Terrifying.

And it has me questioning everything, especially my parenting. When I became a Mum, I had no guidance, no roadmap. There was no one to look up to, no solid ground to stand on. All I knew was this: I had to do everything my mother didn't. That was my compass. And honestly? That wasn't hard.

Fast forward to now my son, nearly 16, has just been made a prefect and sports captain. He's kind, resilient, and full of dreams bigger than the room. My daughter, almost 13, is sharp as a blade, beautiful in her own quiet way, completely at peace in her own company. They are happy. Happy teenagers. And that's when it hits me: I did it. We did it.

I raised them in the long shadow of absence. Their Dad, my husband, has missed more than half of their lives saving the world, while I held the line at home. I raised our children, built a business from scratch, and poured every ounce of myself into something that felt bigger than survival. And now, I'm still standing. Stronger. Wiser. And about to go to Mongolia. Their dad is now going to be around more, no more long tours, no more long stretches away from the UK. Now he will step into my shoes and raise the children. I've never been a selfish parent but is this selfish?

I've always believed the most selfish people make the most exhausted parents. It sounds harsh, maybe, but I've seen it. Again and again. If you're someone who's used to always putting yourself first your needs, your space, your time, then parenting feels like war. A constant tug-of-war between what you want and what your child needs. And usually, the child loses.

For me, it wasn't like that. Parenting came naturally. Giving up sleep, time, comfort, none of it was hard, not when I looked into the eyes of someone who needed me. I've never struggled with sacrifice when love is involved. When I care, I give everything.

But I've also learned how to switch off fully. If someone shows me cruelty, manipulation, or dishonesty if their energy is wrong, I shut down. Empathy off like a light switch. They vanish into fog. Not everyone deserves access to the softest parts of you. And I've learned to protect that.

This isn't just about parenting. It's about partnership. I've learned that love isn't made of big gestures or perfect words, it's made in the hard moments. The late nights. The quiet support. The space you give each other to grow, even when it hurts. Real love sees you. It doesn't ask you to shrink. A bit of advice - stop chasing people who want to meet you halfway.

A Moment of Reckoning. So here I am, standing at the edge of this huge adventure, and part of me feels selfish. I'm leaving them for nearly a month. And that voice in the back of my head whispers: What if you die out there?
It's dramatic. But it's real. That fear. That guilt. That mother-thread tugging at my ankles. But here's the thing I've always told them to follow their dreams. And this is mine. They want me to go. They want time with their Dad. That's never happened before!

They want to see me living. So, I'm going. Because what if I didn't? What would that teach them? That dreams only matter until you have children? That a mother's life stops when theirs begin? No. That's not the legacy I want to leave. This is my time. I'm going and they're watching me do it with pride in their eyes.

Alongside the adventure, I decided to run a fundraiser for the West Search and Rescue team I volunteer with. It's a cause close to my heart. I believe deeply in helping others, and this team does just that: quietly, selflessly, often in the shadows. We need more people like that in the world.

I've managed to raise just under £500 so far (by June 2025), and I'm truly grateful for every single person who's supported the cause. But here's the funny part, and by funny, I mean - ouch. I struggled with getting donations from Simon's network of colleagues and friends. But I guess generosity isn't always a matter of means; it's a matter of mindset. Okay, not all were bad. One lovely man lent me his MSR tent, and one gave me a box of survival meals, so not all bad!

So yeah, it stung a little. But it also reminded me of why I'm doing this: for the people who show up without being asked, who give even when no one's watching. That's who I do it for. That's who I am. And I'll keep giving because that's what makes me feel alive. Even if the stingy beggars never get it.

May is my birthday month and yes, I do a whole month. Not for attention, but to catch up on all the celebrations I never had growing up. I've been making up for lost time for about twenty years now. When birthdays used to mean just not getting hit, any joy you create later becomes a quiet revolution.

I never had parties as a child. I used to dream them instead. Full-on imaginary affairs. Balloons, cakes, music, presents grandparents friends all conjured up in my head while I lay in bed in silence. That's what imagination gave me: survival. Magic out of nothing. So now, as an adult, I throw the kind of birthdays I always needed. And this year, I've got a lot to celebrate!

(Image: anon)

The celebrations kicked off with a wilderness weekend with two of my oldest friends Sarah and Claire. We're like a Celtic coven, the three of us. All with Irish blood, similar hearts. We're on the same frequency, always. Kind, funny, a little feral. That kind of friendship is rare, the kind where you don't need to explain anything. We camped wild, laughed until we wheezed, and remembered who we are when the world is quiet. These two women are soulmates in their own right. I feel lucky to know them.

Next up: the annual Snowdon trip. It's become tradition every year, we gather at the base of the mountain and climb together. This time was extra special. Lou and Cerys came: my chosen family. Lou is one of my best friends, full of fire and strength. Cerys is solid and wise and funny in that quiet way that lands when you least expect it. When things go wrong, you want these two nearby!

Then there's Simon who made it this year after missing the last two. It meant everything to have him there again, walking beside me, laughing with the kids. Speaking of kids, mine come every year, and seeing them up on the mountain with me is one of my life's greatest joys. Three of my brothers showed up this time too: Andy, Jim, and Kev. We all camped together in a high field, swapping stories, eating too much, laughing our heads off. It felt like something real something we'll carry with us.

And my youngest friend, Annabel. She's one of the strongest women I know. She's got athlete energy, a fierce heart, and the kind of drive that changes rooms. She's going places. And I feel lucky to call her a best friend.

We've already booked next year. Same crew. Same magic. The final leg of the celebrations was a little house party back in Hereford, a cosy, 60s-themed night. There was my brothers Sam, Jim and his girlfriend Danielle, my Hereford best friend Katy, Kirsty, Rosa, and a few of Simon's friends. We had music, drinks, silly dancing, and a bit of glam. Nothing over the top. Just that kind of night where you feel like you've landed in the right place, surrounded by people who get you. It was joyful, relaxed, full of laughter.

Now the glitter's settling. The birthday bunting's packed away. The house is quieter, and I'm finally catching up on all the loose ends I let fly during the celebrations. I feel full in the best way. Like I've filled up the tank before I head off to somewhere wild again.

Big Pause: The weekend before I leave

It's early June 2025, the weekend before I leave for Mongolia, and I'm crying. Not in a graceful, cinematic way. I mean full, messy, choking sobs, the kind that leaves your chest raw. It's taken me completely by surprise. I can't even remember the last time I cried like this. Years ago, maybe. Maybe longer.

And it's not because I'm weak. It's not that I'm breaking. I think it's the opposite, I think something inside me is finally softening. Something I locked away a long time ago.

I've just finished delivering one of my Women's Wilderness Weekends. It was beautiful, really beautiful. Our base is perfect: wild camping on a Herefordshire farm beside the River Wye, everything sourced locally, the river singing through the trees. Firelight. Cold swims. Hot food. And laughter so much laughter. I've been running these weekends for a few years now, and I believe in them with everything I've got. They empower women. They reconnect us to the land, to our bodies, to each other.

This group was different. They weren't just attendees. These were women I'd met before on that unforgettable expedition in Sweden that I thought so hard to get on I knew I had to get on this trip back in 2023. We'd paddled wild rivers together, shared sleeping bags and soggy socks and long, soul-bearing talks around the fire. We'd survived together. And through that, we'd bonded in a way that's hard to explain unless you've done it.

So when they arrived this weekend, it wasn't as strangers. It was as friends. And not just any friends the biggest group of real, close female friends I've ever had. That might sound strange, but it's the truth.

Growing up, I learned early on that I didn't belong. I was the weird girl, the one who smelled, the one kids were mean to. I was laughed at, excluded, picked on. That kind of childhood carves deep. It taught me to expect rejection, even when none is coming. It taught me to be careful. To keep my friendships small. One or two people at most. Any more than that and I'd feel swallowed up. Unsafe.

But here's the thing. This weekend, those same women, those beautiful, brilliant women brought me food, asked about me and reassured me about my adventure. It doesn't sound like much, does it? But it was everything.

They cared for me without needing me to perform strength. And that's never happened to me before, not in a group that size. It was the first time I've ever felt truly safe inside a crowd. Not leading it. Not proving myself. Just in it. And loved. And that, I think, is why I cried. Because I felt held. Because I was about to go on the biggest adventure of my life, and this moment reminded me why it matters. Why community matters. Why pushing myself to do scary things is worth it.

That adventure opened something in me. It showed me what connection can feel like, when it's real. That trip built the seed of what I've grown on these weekends, this business, this movement. And now, just days before I fly to Mongolia with my canoe and my dreams, these same women showed up to remind me of where it all began.

(Image: selfie)

They reminded me that I'm not doing this alone. That made me think for the first time that I'm not alone. Mongolia is calling. And I'm ready to go. And one last thing: to all the close friends who know me well, who've camped with me, climbed mountains with me, danced in my kitchen or sat by a fire laughing till we cried. If this is the first time you're hearing pieces of my past, I just want to say this: I didn't hide it from you. I just didn't think it needed to take up space between us.

I built my life forward brick by brick and most days, I've chosen joy over explanation. But as I write this, as I tell the truth more openly, I realise there's power in sharing. Not for sympathy. Not for shock. But so you understand the full shape of the woman beside you.

I've survived things I never thought I would. And now I celebrate hard, love fiercely, and live loudly not just in spite of what I came from, but because of it. Thank you for walking beside me all these years. Whether you knew the full story or not, your love held me anyway.

Chapter 5: Departure

Travelling got me thinking. There's over eight billion people in this world. And I'm just one. We are just one. We are one. Does that make me special? Does that make you special? Does that make it special?

I guess that's a question you should be asking yourself. To me, this is special. This is why I left my children. This is why I left my husband. This is why I chose this adventure over all the others.

Three weeks. It's the longest I've ever been away. And I don't mean from people, I mean from them: my children. The people who are my world. It's been hours and it's already tearing me apart.

He's the one who always leaves with military work, long tours, long stretches. I've stayed. They've stayed. And now it's me who's leaving and it feels different.

There's a voice whispering:

"Run. Go back. You can't do this. It's too dangerous."

And maybe that voice isn't wrong. Part of me just wants to go home, sit on the sofa, do nothing. Be safe. Be still. Be simple.

Why can't I be that person? Why can't I just be the housewife, clean, cook, and the highlight of my day being the school run? And yet when I try to hold that life in my hands, it slips through. Because I know I can be that woman. But I'm not only her. I'm also this: A woman who chose something bold. A woman walking into risk, into meaning, into a story.

My husband noticed I was struggling, anxious, and finding it really hard to leave the children and him as it's normally the other way round. He looked me in the eyes. They were deep blue. Strong eyes that could kill you. One stare. He really does have those eyes if people know him, you know what I mean, the look. His look.

And he said to me:

> "All your life, Rose, you've been looking after people. Doing what's best for them. Putting them before your own needs. Now this is the time for you. To do something for yourself. And this is just a gate that's gonna open a lot of doors for you. You are a truly incredible woman, selfless, kind, caring, adventurous, fierce and truly amazing. This is why you need to do this. And

you're gonna come back. We're gonna be right here. And you're gonna start doing things for yourself".

Wow. What a man.

I'm not just one in eight billion. I'm this one. Right now. That's so many people, but there's so many lonely, strange when you think about it. And strange that I've decided to give up my whole life for Mongolia for this adventure to find something in me, to be there more for my children and my husband, to be a better person, to be more whole. Do you think I will find it? We'll have to wait and see.

Well, that went smoothly. I left the house at 3am. Quiet. Heavy. I kissed the kids, kissed Simon, told them I love them, so much more than they'll ever know. Then I was off to Swindon to see my brother. It's our tradition, really. He always takes me to the airport.

My baby brother, Jim. I call him Jim Jim. I've been like a second Mum to him, ever since the day he arrived, unplanned, unwanted, and somehow already chilled out.

Life didn't give him an easy start. The odds were against us both. But here's the twist, he didn't become another statistic. Jim didn't turn to crime or chaos. He built something. He's now a company director. He owns his own house. He found love. He found life. He's proof that where you start doesn't have to be where you end up. That kindness, generosity, and care can survive anything, can thrive, even. We didn't have much growing up, but we've both always given back. That's just who we are.

Anyway, back to it. Thirteen hours, two flights, and a blink-and-you-miss-it changeover. No chaos. No drama. I just did it. And here's the strange bit. The plane? The plane is the only place I ever really stop.

At home, I'm always moving. Always doing. Always ticking something off. On the ground, there's always someone to care for, something to fix, somewhere to be.

But on a plane? There's nothing else I can do. I can't jump off. I can't change course. I just have to sit. And think. Which is something I don't often let myself do. It's hard for me, that stillness. But it's also oddly relaxing. Because I've got no choice in the matter. No expectations. No distractions. Just air under my feet and time in my hands. Strange, isn't it? That 30,000 feet in the air is the only place I feel grounded.

Interlude: introducing 'The Gang'

(Image: selfie)

We all met for the first time today.

Matt, the leader. 'The kindest man in the world', I wrote in my notes. And I meant it. I already love him. Not in a romantic way, of course, but in a best friend vibes, I'd-trust-you-with-my-life kind of way.

Then there's Deb, the other woman on this trip. It's just me and Deb, so we've already bonded as the Girl Gang. She's lived, she's laughed, she's got loads of life experience and the kind of presence that makes you want to sit near her and soak some of it in.

Her husband is here too. I can't remember his name yet (I'll get there), so for now he's just Deb's husband. (Turns out it's Kev). But he's kind and clever sharp, in that quiet way and I'm already looking forward to hearing his stories around the campfire. He's that guy who's seen a lot of energy. I reckon he'll have some good ones when we light our first yak poo fire. (Yes. Really. Yak poo.)

Davaaka, our guide, will be part of that too. But more on him later.

Then there's Mark. He's good with his hands, he made that clear right away and has this calm, quiet way about him. Like he's spent time figuring out the world and how people tick. He's protective too. I noticed that. Protective in a gentle, watchful way.

Next is Nick. He's just cool. Loves his family. Loves his kit. Has the best gear. And he's funny like, properly funny, not trying-too-hard funny. He's also into history, which I love. I think we're going to get on well. I get the sense he's steady.

And finally, Chris. Chris has just retired, and honestly? I think he might be one of the happiest men in the world. He's got the most joyful personality; he hasn't got a negative bone in his body. He's positive, smart, and colourful. I like him and feel very safe in this company.

Chapter 6: First day in Mongolia

It's our first day in Mongolia and I'm wide awake, overthinking everything. I keep wondering about the river. What's it going to be like? Will it be gravelly or deep and slick with silt? Will it roar? Will it whisper? Are my paddling skills actually up to standard, or have I convinced myself of something I can't deliver?

Will the wind be so strong it throws me straight out of my canoe? Will I capsize? What about the fish? Are they really going to be that big? Like, eat-a-person big? Okay. I might be spiralling a bit now. That last one is... unlikely. Very unlikely. (Or is it?)

It was Culture Day.

Me: "Museums? Yes, yes, yes!"

Ever since I was a little girl, I've been obsessed with museums. I remember being in primary school when they'd announce a school trip. You needed a permission slip and a bit of money. But if it cost anything, I knew I wouldn't be going.

The people I lived with would either laugh, rip up the form in front of me, or burn it. School books too. Gone as soon as I brought them home. Sometimes torn to pieces. Sometimes stuffed in the bin like they meant nothing. Eventually, the school stopped sending them with me altogether. No forms. No books. I suppose they just thought I was careless or naughty. No one ever asked why I never brought anything back. But I remember.

I remember the shame of not being able to go. The silence. The fear of asking. It wasn't just about a trip. It was about being allowed to learn, to explore, to exist outside of control. Because that's what it was. Control. Education is freedom, and I was kept from it.

So now, every chance I get to go to a museum, I go. And I have the best time ever. Because I can. Because no one can rip that away from me anymore. So when the opportunity came to visit the museums in Ulaanbaatar, I was first out the door. I spent hours wandering the grand corridors of the Chojin Lama Temple Museum, once a working monastery and now home to breathtaking Buddhist artwork and history. Then I visited the Gandantegchinlen Monastery, still active and rich with spiritual energy, where I saw monks chanting and a towering statue of Avalokiteśvara, the bodhisattva of compassion.

I stood before the Golden Genghis Khan at the Genghis Khan Museum. The place was filled with stunning artefacts that told the story of Mongolia's warrior-king, not just as a conqueror, but as a visionary leader of a vast empire.

And then there was the silver giant himself. The Genghis Khan Equestrian Statue at Tsonjin Boldog. The largest equestrian statue in the world. Forty metres of steel rising out of the steppe like a mirage. I climbed to the top of the horse's head and looked out over the land. It took my breath away. This wasn't just a statue. It was a symbol of power, resilience, and pride. The kind I'd been denied growing up.

(Image: Rosemary)

This was the museum trip of my dreams, but Saint Fagans in South Wales is still my top five of course! After the museums, we boarded a small plane to Mörön in northern Mongolia. The plane was so small and fully packed.

We stayed with a local family, and I spent some time hanging out with the younger girls. They were incredible, sweet, smart, and so fluent in English it amazed me. The youngest, only five years old, gave me a big hug the moment I arrived. So cute. So open. So full of light.

Then came the journey. We climbed into a Soviet-built VAZ 452 van, known as the UAZik or just 'The Loaf' because it looks like a squashed tin loaf of bread. This clunky, legendary beast bounced over boulders and dust tracks, charging headfirst into the wilderness like it had done it all before. No tarmac. No road signs. No barriers. Just wild Mongolia, open and vast.

We rumbled across ridge lines and riverbeds, carving through valleys that looked like they hadn't changed in thousands of years. The landscapes felt raw and sacred, like the Earth had only just been born here. We crossed rivers, the water surging around the van's wheels, climbed steep mountain trails with no tracks at all, just instinct and horsepower. I clung on for dear life, wide-eyed and breathless.

This was scarier than anything I've ever done on UK roads. I'll never complain about a narrow lane in Herefordshire again. We passed herds of animals, camels, goats, horses, cows and yaks. The skies were filled with black kites, gliding in huge circles above us, sometimes hundreds at a time. We saw swans drifting across mirror-still lakes and eagles perched on rocky outcrops like gatekeepers of the land.

The mountains in northern Mongolia were unlike anything I've ever seen. They weren't just tall. They were alive. Formed from ancient granite and sandstone, the rock faces were worn by wind and ice and time itself. Deep crevices and natural arches carved into the sides made them look like sculptures, like faces of old gods watching us from above. Some ridgelines looked like sleeping giants. Others opened into massive caves and holes, as if the land had exhaled and left its lungs behind. Mist clung to the valleys like breath, and everywhere was green, lush, endless green broken only by wildflowers and white river ribbons.

This was not a landscape that whispers. It roars. It thunders. It hums with memory. It reminds you how small you are and how big life can feel.

After five hours driving we made it to our start point at Bayanzurkh village, then set up our first camp. We unpacked and pitched the so-called pop-up tents, though I wouldn't use the word 'pop' with all the holes involved. Still, I found it easy. I've done this so many times now, it felt like second nature. And compared to my usual bivvy bag, this was a five-star hotel. Luxury. We set up our little portable fire. Yes, really. We carry it in our canoe. It's brilliant.

Dinner: tuna pasta. Five-star cuisine. And of course, we opened the vodka. The Mongolian way. You dip your wedding finger into the vodka. If it's poisoned, the silver ring will change colour. You flick a drop to the sky, a nod to Genghis Khan's grandfather who was poisoned, and then you say: Togar. Togar that's what it sounds like probably not the correct spelling. Turns out it's Togha!

Later in my tent I sorted out my kit so I could be more organized. People say I bring too many socks. I say: warm feet, warm heart. You can never have too many socks.

And of course, my first aid kit. The holy trinity: head, stomach, feet. If I get a headache or fever, I can cool myself down. If I get stomach issues, I've got Immodium or Gaviscon. If I get blisters, I've got plasters. That's my first aid Bible.

With everything tucked around me, I lay back, listening to horses grazing by the river. I was wrapped in warmth, in the quiet power of a good day, a good place. Heaven. Good night.

Chapter 7: River Delgermörön

Day one on the river. The weather kept shifting. Patches of rain, then bursts of sunshine. The temperature hovered around 15 to 20 degrees. It felt alive, like the river itself was already testing us.

(Image: Chris)

After a good night's sleep, we packed up and got straight on the water. As soon as we got in, two minutes later Kev and Deb capsized, it was clear Kev and Deb weren't very technical when it came to whitewater. I think they were just as shocked as Matt was. But the great thing about that moment? It gave us a chance to do some rescues. And honestly, I thought it was fun. We learnt techniques, we threw lines, we emptied boats, and I loved every minute of it.

Later, when we stopped, Deb spoke to me. She said she didn't think the water would be like this. She's used to the River Dee. Calmer. Gentler. She and Kev do a lot of paddling together, but not this kind of water. Not this kind of challenge. They're used to romantic paddling trips, locking through Scotland together, flat calm stretches. They've got rhythm as a couple, but this river has no rhythm you can count on.

Flat water paddling and whitewater are two completely different beasts. I think Deb expected stillness, and maybe to walk around any rapids. But today was full of rapids. And they fell in. Quite a few times. She was nervous. Frightened. And I get it. It is extreme. But I did my best to help, to reassure her. I gave her encouragement, told her she could do this. Reminded her we were all here to support each other. She appreciated that. She really did.

The rescue work was exciting. We were throwing lines, running in lines, emptying boats, tracking. At one point, the leader made the call to walk around the next rapid. I agreed. One of the other boats had just capsized. Chris and Mark. I think it was because they weren't kneeling when they hit the whitewater. That's just my opinion, but I've never seen anyone paddle whitewater without kneeling. You need low gravity. A steady base. You need to be in control. If you're too high in the boat, you're unstable. And they were. They went in and came out shocked

I wanted to ask Kev and Deb why they'd chosen something this extreme when whitewater wasn't their thing. But I didn't ask. Maybe they've got their reasons. Maybe we all do. It's only day one. The only way is up, or downstream in our case. The only thing we can do now is improve, build trust, become a team.

Today we only managed to paddle 20 kilometres. We were supposed to cover 40. That means we're going to have to make it up somehow in the coming days. I knew this river would be hard. I was scared, too. The rapids here are uncharted, it's serious water. And we're in a completely unmapped area. No one's ever properly charted this river. There's nothing out there. Just rumours, old satellite images, and gut instinct.

I'm so glad I trained. If I hadn't, I'd be struggling too. The training paid off. The hard work paid off. It's funny. I thought I'd be the worst in the group. The least experienced. I had all those doubts before coming here. But actually I'm okay. I don't know why I doubted myself. I can do this. I've got this. And it's so exciting. River Delgermörön, I'm going to complete you.

We're all in unknown territory. There's no escape route. No emergency team waiting. No one's coming to rescue us. There's no turning back now. We're in this together. The only way through is forward. Together.

After battling the rapids and rescuing each other, we finally reached our first campsite. We'd only covered half the planned distance, but we made it. The site was beautiful, set high, overlooking the hills across the river. The mountains in the distance looked like a stegosaurus spine. Jagged. Ancient. It was unreal. I've never seen anything like it in my life.

We had to put up the folding stone tents. Heavy and awkward. We were all exhausted, but we got them up. We had to. No one else was going to do it for us.

We gathered around the fire. Matt made spam curry. He's a brilliant cook. Outdoor food is never glamorous, especially when you're guiding or living in the wild. It's not about taste. It's about fuel. Everything's dry, packed, rationed. Light to carry. Heavy with calories. Most of it tastes like nothing, or worse. But it gets the job done.

(Image: Chris)

And you've got to be careful. Food and water out here can turn on you. You don't want the squits in the middle of the Mongolian wilderness. We filter river water, then boil it, just to be safe.

I'm putting the pen down now. My arms are heavy. My bones ache. Tomorrow will be harder. I can feel it. I wonder what Matt's thinking after the day we had. All those rescues. All those flips. He must have a million risk assessments running through his head right now.

Then it was day two on the river. We managed 27 kilometres today, seven more than yesterday. Still not hitting the numbers we need, but a little progress is better than none. Kev and Deb had another wobble. We were approaching the start of a grade 3 section. As soon as the water got technical, they were straight in. Again. It was hard to watch.

I love Deb and Kev, I really do. And I was hoping, really hoping, they'd have a better day. I didn't want to see them go in again. But whitewater doesn't wait for hope. It was like paddling through a graveyard of stone. Rocks everywhere, unpredictable, shifting under the current. To move through it safely, you need real skill. And even then, luck. Honestly, it was like nothing I've ever seen before. Even the most experienced paddlers would've struggled. Would've had to get out, line up, and walk around it. So that's what we did. The leader made the call: line it and walk it, for safety.

We spent two hours near those rapids, soaked and on edge. The rain wouldn't stop. The cold was creeping in. Everyone was tired, dripping, silent. We'd reached that place where bodies start to shut down if you don't get dry and fed. Matt made the decision to set up camp early.

It was a good call. We moved fast, getting tents up in the rain. The routine helps. Everyone knows their bit now. We're learning the rhythm of discomfort, how to keep going when your boots squelch and your fingers sting. We wolfed down a meal-in-a-bag and hit the sack.

Now I'm lying in my tent. Rain tapping on the canvas. Everything damp, but manageable. And I can't stop thinking about how much I love not having signal. No phone. No pings. No distractions. No scrolling. Just my diary, my thoughts, and the river. Some photos. Some scribbled notes.

It's been amazing. No emails. No texts. No YouTube. No social media. And yes of course I worry. About my kids. About my husband. About what might happen while I'm out here in the middle of nowhere. But I have faith in him. I really do. He's got this. And anyway, what could I do from here?

There is no rushing to help anyone right now. There's no 'just popping home'. I'm not reachable. And I'm finally okay with that. Because right now, I'm doing something for myself.

All my life, I've done things for everyone else. Loved hard. Worked harder. Cared until I had nothing left. And now? Now I'm doing this. For me. Not worrying about anyone else. Not caretaking. Not organising. Not covering. Just surviving. Breathing. Paddling. Sleeping. Eating. Me. And it's strange. And it's hard. But it's also new. And powerful. And necessary.

Chapter 8: The weight of water

The weather is starting to bite now, 32 degrees Celsius today, the heat bouncing off the water, thick and heavy. We covered 42 kilometres. That's no small feat when you're dragging loaded canoes and your body's already running on less-than-usual sleep and food.

Packing up in the morning was brutal: the sun already glaring down, and the kit felt twice as heavy as usual. Canoeing with heavy boats is a different game altogether. You can't just chuck gear in and hope for the best. Every kilo has to be balanced, weight placed just so to avoid capsizing, and every paddle stroke feels like you're dragging the earth behind you. We did a full portage around a set of graveyard rapids. There was a sheer mountain on one side of the river and tucked into its base, a dark mouth of rock where the current disappeared. Matt called it right: that cave would eat a canoe and never spit it back out.

"Death", he said simply. So we carried everything. No shortcuts.

The river feels ancient. Like it knows things. It snakes through the valleys like it's choosing its own fate, brushing past boulders and cliffs with this quiet authority. On either side, the mountains rise up like silent sentries, watching, unmoving. When the river narrows, it's like entering another realm. Something out of Lord of the Rings jagged cliffs, mist curling off the water, silence so deep you can hear your breath.

The team really came together. We lifted, hauled, sweated. I love those moments when no one's complaining, just doing the job. Soon as we relaunched, Deb looked rattled, and Matt, who notices everything, shifted canoe pairings. He took Deb in his boat to help her steady, pairing her husband Kev with Nick. I think he did it to quietly give her back some control after two tough days.

So now it's: Matt and Deb; Kev and Nick; Chris and Mark; me and Davaaka. And I'm so glad I'm with him.

Davaaka is one of the most grounded people I've ever met. A man of few words, but when he speaks, it matters. He works like a machine, has this funny humour I wasn't expecting, and a love for Mongolia that shines from his face.We're sharing language he's teaching me words in Mongolian and I'm teaching him swear words from back home.

He thinks my paddling is decent he said so with a nod today, and honestly, that nod meant more than a thousand compliments. He's got that rare energy that says, I see you. And I feel it. We're in sync. He's started opening up more, while we paddled in silence, he spoke softly about his childhood. His father left when he was young, and he was raised by his mother in a quiet village.

"She gave me everything," he said, not looking at me. "She carried the whole weight. She is strong like the mountains."

There was such reverence in his voice, it hit me deep. It's a strange, grounding bond, that kind of mutual respect for where we came from. We paddled on in silence after that, but it wasn't empty. It felt full.

(Image: Chris)

When we finally pulled into camp, we built a fire, gathered wood, started drying everything from the day before. Mark strung up a line and we all hung out our soaked gear like wild nomads with a laundry obsession. The sun worked its magic. No one capsized. No one even fell in. That's a good day.

We haven't had to use the yak poo yet, there's been enough decent wood around to make do. But I'm weirdly looking forward to seeing how it works. Adventure isn't just paddling or the Instagram highlight reel. It's hard graft. It's blisters and wet socks and heavy lifting. You don't just "do the activity" you set up camp, carry heavy loads, cook from scratch, ration your food, and wash in cold water. You go hungry sometimes. You ache. You bleed. And you keep going.

It always makes me laugh, those glossy ads for outdoor gear, where everyone's shiny and clean. I've never seen a woman on expedition look like that past Day One. Where are the calloused hands? The sunburnt cheeks? The arguments over firewood?

This stuff is real. And I think we need more real in the world. I'm starting to feel the toll though. My hands are blistered, now the skin splitting at the base of my thumbs, raw from hours gripping the paddle. But weirdly, I don't mind. It's like my body's building itself up, thickening where it needs to. Still, I have to watch the fatigue. The heat hits, hard it's not just temperature, it's weight.

And water: water is everything. You don't just grab a bottle when you're thirsty. You have to plan. Find it, filter it, boil it. Cool it. Wait. It's work, even just to stay hydrated. Drink, drink, drink: I repeat it to myself like a mantra. I can't afford to crash out here.

Tonight, around the fire, someone asked me how I met Simon. And I just couldn't. I said:

"I'm sorry. I can't talk about it. Not here. Not yet".

Because that story is a war and a wonder all in one. We met in a time of chaos, in a chapter I haven't made peace with. And retelling it still makes my chest close up. One day, I'll share it. But not on this trip. Not while I need to keep my head clear and my emotions tight. I simply said:

"Maybe another time," and smiled my way out of it.

But after that, I couldn't stop thinking about him. And here's the thing I've realised out here, alone on the other side of the world, on this river that never stops moving: yes, I am a woman who needs a man. I can lift heavy things. I can paddle for miles. I can survive off-grid with no mirror, no makeup, no hot water. But I need my man behind me. He makes me stronger. I am a woman who loves fiercely and unapologetically.

Simon is the wolf in my life, my tether and my echo. The father of our Wolfpack. We've grown up together, built a life from nothing, raised two strong children, bought a house with money we saved, stayed out of debt, kept pushing forward. We've built something real, something rare. And even though we've both missed each other's birthdays over the years the life we live demands that sometimes this one is a different hit. Because I'm the one who's away now. And I can feel the ache of that distance in my bones.

He's 40 today. My action man. In every way. Even his stubbornness is endearing, especially because he's rarely wrong. He's solid, steady, honest, hardworking, and so damn handsome. Honestly, his body looks like something you'd find in a comic bookstore labelled "limited edition." But it's his mind and his heart that make him mine. I respect the hell out of him. We've made each other better. We've held each other up. We've built a love story no one else needed to understand, just us.

I had a moment earlier, just a flash of our last night before I flew out. Lying in bed with Simon, the weight of his arm across me, skin on skin. The quiet rhythm of his breath, the rise and fall of his chest. I remember tracing the scar on his chin; he got this from the night we met, just letting my fingers map the familiar landscape of him.

"You'll smash it," he whispered. "But don't be a hero. Come home."

(Image: Roman)

So strange him saying them, my words to me when it's normally my words to him. God, I miss him! We've done well, come so far. We've made it through storms. We may be apart in body but not in soul! I've never felt more close to him. And tonight, as the fire cracks and everyone's drifting off to sleep, I'm holding that truth close.

Chapter 9: Echoes in the gut

Another relentlessly hot day on the river. There's a feeling brewing in my gut, a quiet hum that tells me I'm part of something truly exceptional. This river: hardly anyone dares to use it. It's like the current itself is nurturing its own wildness. Mongolians don't canoe. They don't navigate their rivers the way we do; they often don't even swim. A lot of them are scared of the water, and too many lives are claimed by its currents, making it something to be feared.

There are, perhaps, only four canoes in all of Mongolia, and by some incredible twist of fate, we have them. We're the sole four vessels cutting through these untouched waters. And my canoe partner, Dakaavka, is the only Mongolian to have ever kayaked the Mediterranean Sea. Think about that: canoeing is virtually unheard of here. It truly makes this expedition feel sacred, a privilege.

(Image: Mark)

Being a woman on this river, having this unparalleled opportunity, amplifies that feeling. For all the women out there with adventure in their hearts, I hope my story ignites something inthem, pushes them to step out and claim their own wild. I'd love to set up a trip, female-only. It would be extraordinary.

Speaking of feelings in my stomach, it's a little off today. These processed, packed travel meals, they're safe, yes, but they don't sit right. They're fuel, a necessary evil, but a far cry from the balanced diet I've painstakingly built for myself over the years.

It took me decades to truly learn how to eat. As a child, food was never a given. You ate when you could, a desperate scramble for calories. Thank God for free school meals; I'd go back for seconds, thirds: they saved me. I learned to pick and forage out of necessity, but a proper diet? Nutritional understanding? That was alien.

The first time I ever stepped into a restaurant, I was sixteen. I was with my granny, utterly overwhelmed, a wild animal set loose in a strange new world. I ended up throwing food everywhere, just crying for help without knowing how to ask. I still look back at that day with a pang of regret for embarrassing her.

My granny wasn't often around, though just before I turned sixteen, she became a lifeline, finally asking the questions I desperately needed someone to ask. Before that, I was largely left to my own devices. She had her own burdens, primarily caring for her severely ill son, my uncle, who was schizophrenic, had MS, and a history of severe drug abuse. Those challenges consumed her.

Our daily food on this Mongolian river adventure looks something like this: morning, hot water and oats. Porridge, fortified with walnuts and a squeeze of jam. Snack, an oat bar or a square of chocolate. I always have an allowance for chocolate, even if it means ditching clothes. I carry a bar for every day, and yes, I share with those who need it. Lunch, boiling water in our jet boilers, then soup with bread we've made earlier from just flour and water. Another oat bar and some sweets to keep our sugars up. Dinner is a simple boil-in-the-bag meal with hot water.

If I'd had this menu as a kid, I would have been over the moon. This is pure luxury. But now, as a grown woman with a deep understanding of nutrition, I know it's just fuel. It sustains us, but it's not optimal. I guess I've become a bit obsessive about what I eat, but after years of deprivation, I have the choice now. I want my body strong, healthy, and capable. Most of our money goes on food: the irony isn't lost on me that eating healthy is often far more expensive.

But out here, on this river, I feel like one of the luckiest people alive. To be invited, to secure a spot on this adventure: *me*. I was picked. I was accepted. I am good enough. They like me around.

With every mile I paddle, I'm immersed in the sheer, undeniable beauty of the world. Everything simply *is*, and everything has a purpose. This journey has become a deep well of reflection, reminding me of everything I've faced, how strong I've become, and how truly resilient I am.

Yet, I just want to leave the hard times behind. To heal the scars, inside and out. To heal my body, my soul, and to stop waking up expecting the worst. I don't want to live like every day is my last anymore. That frantic need to survive, that hyper-vigilance, it's exhausting. I need to live like I'm going to see tomorrow. Like I'm going to see you tomorrow, next week, next year. I don't know why this constant specter of death haunts me, unless it's precisely because I don't want to die. I want to live.

When I was eight, and again at thirteen, I tried to take my life. I simply couldn't bear it anymore. It's a terrifying thought, but thankfully, I didn't know how to do it. Otherwise, I wouldn't be writing this book today. Those times were utterly dark, excruciatingly hard. So, to anyone out there who has ever felt that despair: things *do* get better. They always do. I won't go into the details here, but I am an incredibly lucky woman. And sadly, no one raised an eyebrow back then. No one saved me. I had to save myself. And I did. I ran away just before my sixteenth birthday.

And that's why I want to live. And choose to live. Because I know, intimately, what it's like to truly want to die. So if I can choose life after knowing true darkness, I believe anyone can. I have seen evil and been in its presence.

Chapter 10: Nomadic families

We saw our first nomadic Mongolian family. We stopped in our canoes by the riverside, and they invited all eight of us in. There was an old man, around 85, still working the farm, and his wife, who was very kind. They took us in while looking after their young children, there must have been about four of them.

(Image: Matt)

The lady sat us down in their home to cook rice. We all sat on the other side as she gave us warm milk curds and anything else they made from their animals' milk. It was a very different taste; I'd never had anything like it. They also made this natural yogurt stuff, which was quite nice, and these biscuits that looked like yumyums, made from milk. They didn't taste like them, though! It's rude not to take the food they offer, so I tried everything, just a little bit. I don't really drink milk products at home, so my tummy gets a little bit upset, but I just took it, smiled, and drank as much as I could without being rude.

The children's parents were outside working with the animals. The kind old lady spoke to us, and we had an advocate translating for us. We thanked her, and she welcomed us. We explained that we don't have this in the UK, people don't really let you into their homes and feed you. And then she replied, "We are all humans. We will share our stuff with you". That was the wisest thing I've ever heard. What a wonderful woman. What a way of living, how they just accept everyone and look after everyone in their home.

Their movable houses, called *gers*, were fascinating. There's a stove in the middle, and from the stove, two posts identify the man and woman in the marriage. You must never walk between these two posts, as it's considered bad luck. That was interesting to learn, and everything they had in their home, they offered us. I'm not sure what animal milk it was, I don't think it was cow's. It was quite overwhelming. Nick got emotional; he has a sensitive soul. I love seeing his passion for life and people. He's a really warm, kind guy.

Anyway, we all nodded our heads to the lady and thanked her. We tried to talk to the children, but it was just smiles and glances, and the lady just kept saying:

"Eat! Eat! Eat!"

We gave the kids sweets and small toys that we had bought along with us, just in case this happened, and I'm glad we did. They were so grateful, and it was so cute. We got back on our boat and said:

"Bayartai", which means goodbye in Mongolian.

(Image: Chris)

Once we reached the campsite after a few more kilometres of paddling, we had covered a good amount today on the river. For now, let's talk about camp. We're all getting quite settled in now, setting up really quickly. We're in a routine, in a groove; we know what goes up first and what goes where, and our tents are getting closer together. We are becoming a family, so we had more time sitting around chilling after other things were done earlier.

Me, Chris, and Nick went for a dip. The water was refreshing, and it was wild. It wasn't very deep where we washed, but it was enough to have a quick wash. Afterward, Nick delivered a yoga session for us. This was amazing. It was just me, Nick, and Chris. It was a good session.

After it, a tear came over me. It was the weirdest thing ever. I don't do yoga; it's too slow for me, and I need to keep moving. But it was the way Nick was talking to us. His kindness was oozing out of him in abundance. Anyway, it made me feel like I wish he were my Dad. He was the Dad I should have had. Actually I'm surrounded by Dad figures here; all of them. Mark, Chris, Matt, Kev, Nick, any of them could be my Dad. Okay, maybe not Matt, he's definitely too young to be my Dad. He's more like a mate or a brother. But honestly, I would've been happy with any of these men as a Dad.

This is my dreamworld, and a dreamworld it is. And actually, I've got a Mum here too. Debs is like a Mum; I'd be happy if Debs was my Mum. She's probably the best Mum ever. Anyway, that's enough of that daydreaming, it's back to reality. I guess yoga did open up my mind.

Afterward, we all had a shot of whiskey. It's funny the things you carry when you shouldn't carry much. We all made sure there was space for a bottle of whiskey and a bottle of vodka. Priorities, right? Later, after another boil-in-a-bag meal, the fire was going strong and the whiskey was poured. This time, we did a toast: 'Sláinte!'

Chapter 11: The longest, hardest day

Today was the hardest day yet. In the end, we covered over 60 kilometres, a massive push that tested everyone. What's funny is that our Mongolian guide, Davaaka, wasn't entirely sure how far we'd be going. First he said it might be 20 kilometres, then 40, and by the time we pulled in, it turned out to be 60. It became a bit of a joke. He says "maybe" a lot, and you never quite know what maybe means. I guess it's part of the culture relaxed, flexible, just get on with it. I respect that. It keeps things light.

It was an absolutely beautiful stretch of river. The cliffs turned red, the bends were wild and quiet, and for long moments it was just me, the paddle, and that steady, familiar pull of the current. I enjoyed every moment of it.

And physically? I actually felt amazing. I didn't feel tired at all. I've been training for this for months and months, and I could feel that preparation carrying me. Unlike some of the others, I felt ready. My body was strong. This is why it's so important to train properly when you show up for a physical challenge like this, you want to enjoy it, not just survive it. I honestly could've done another 60 kilometres.

The only thing that got to me was the heat. It was fierce, heavy on the skin, relentless in the air. But I was prepared. I don't mess around with the sun. I dipped my clothes in river water and draped them over my head and body. I was completely covered head to toe with just my eyes poking out. I looked ridiculous, but I stayed cool. I was wary of the sun and respected it. Out here, you have to.

Near the middle of the day, the water slowed right down. What had been 12 km/h currents dropped to 6 km/h, which meant a lot more paddling. And just when it felt like we'd been pushing all day, something else happened.

Rescue time! Me and Davaaka helped with another rescue: this time it was Mark and Chris. They didn't get down on their knees in time, hit a rock, and tipped. Davaaka and I were in the last canoe and reacted fast. We paddled over, threw them a line, tried to get them safe.

I actually felt excited when it happened, not in a bad way, but because I was ready. This is what I've trained for. I love learning, and I love the opportunity to help. So when I threw the line to Mark, I expected him to take it.

But he was reluctant, almost defiant. I don't know if it was because I'm a woman or if it was just pride or shock, but it felt like my help was unwanted. He swam to the edge on his own, and maybe he was fine, but I still think if someone throws you a rescue line, you take it. That's how safety works. That's what we're out here to do: help each other. I don't know what it was, but something in that moment stuck with me. I wonder if he was embarrassed. Or if the idea of being pulled out by me bruised something in him.

What baffles me most is that they didn't go down on their knees. You have to in whitewater. This river isn't beginner-friendly you need to be switched on the entire time. Kneeling gives you control, flexibility, power. You need to read the water constantly and be ready for technical moves. The moment you relax too much, you're at risk. I've been paddling onmy knees most of the time, and they're starting to feel it now sore and numb. But that's what it takes. You do what the river demands.

By now, we've paddled over 160 kilometres, and counting. That hit me today just how far we've come. And I still feel full of energy. There's so much more left in me. The days ahead might not be as technical, but they'll still be long, and I know I can do them.

I'm honestly blown away by Deb and Kev. They might not be the most technical paddlers, but they're so strong. They just go. And go. And go. I haven't heard them complain once about the distance. As long as the water's not too tricky, they can keep going all day. That kind of endurance is something I really admire.

Mark and Chris have paddled before, they've got experience, especially Mark. He loves pack rafting, but even he says it's nothing like this. A canoe, especially an overweight one, is a totally different beast.

Matt and Nick are in the lead canoe. They're like the lookout team, scanning for hazards, calling the lines. Matt, especially, needs to see what's ahead. There's a lot of pressure on him making sure we all follow the right path. I reckon he must be having kittens sometimes.

The group was loud today, the kind of loud that comes from being hot, hungry, and physically tested. Voices carried down the river, sometimes light, sometimes tense. But I stayed positive, keeping spirits high. That's what I do. I kept telling everyone:

"You've got this," and "We're smashing it," and "Keep going!"

I wanted to keep morale high, maybe a bit too high. I sometimes wonder if it comes across as patronising, especially since I'm younger than most of the others. I've got all this energy, and they're exhausted, and maybe I seem too much. But that's just me, I care, and I want us to get through together. I want everyone to feel strong, even when they're not.

When we finally pulled into camp, it felt like we were stepping into a dream. A place called Tultiin Tokhoi Camp, nestled right by the river. It was incredible. The first place we've stayed with a shower.

(Image: Chris)

There were people there. A little shop. We had no idea this was coming, it was a total surprise. I think Davaaka and Matt must've arranged it for us. We all needed it, even if we hadn't said so aloud. The shower felt unreal hot water on tired muscles, the smell of soap, washing off days of sweat and grit. It was a small thing, but also everything. Unfortunately, I couldn't get the mats out of my hair so I had to roll with it. We filled our bellies, relaxed in the shade, and crashed into bed after one of the longest days yet. 60 kilometres behind us. We were shattered, but proud.

Chapter 12: True colours

32 kilometres on the river. The river started to open up, and so did the group. Some people's true colours are showing, people aren't always working together. I reflect, hold my head and get on with things. I was upset by this, but I try and listen and know that not all of us have the same personalities. I've always struggled to be part of groups when I'm not leading them. It's easier to hold space than to take it. When I'm in charge, I know who I am. I'm strong, capable, grounded. I'm useful. But when I'm in a group? When I'm just another woman in the circle, without a job title or a purpose to shield me? That's where I feel uncomfortable.

Anyway, we arrived at our campsite. We sorted ourselves and started to see more people, little farmers' kids and stone structures. In the evening, our campsite looked out over empty pieces of land with a few trees and a hillside bank on the other side of the river.

Then we spotted a cow across the river so mid-rescue, Davaaka, Chris, Matt, and Nick saved it by pulling it up the bank. The nomadic family came to help and they saved that poor cow. It was stuck, collapsed on its side, its legs buckled beneath it so tired it tried to drown itself in the river. It kept going further and further down. The calf was pacing, calling out. For a moment, it looked like the mother wouldn't make it. But the guys didn't give up. They pushed, they pulled, they grunted and slipped in the mud.

Against all odds, they got that cow up. It wasn't quite standing yet, but the next day it was and the baby calf was still by its side. It was heartbreaking to hear that calf cry. In Mongolia, saving an animal is a heroic act. People say it brings good fortune. I'm so proud of our team. That night, we were heroes.

The family was so grateful. They invited us over to say thank you. We all went, and they served us warm milk, cured biscuits, and yoghurt.

They had six children. One of them just two months old had so much hair, he looked at least a year old. I wanted to scoop him up and take him home with me. The Ger was small and warm, full of the smells of milk and earth and woodsmoke.

The older children watched us shyly, clutching bowls of yoghurt, while the younger ones climbed in and out of the doorway like it was a game. There was something so ordinary about it so alive and yet so completely different from everything I know. No screens, no toys, just each other. And they were content.

(Image: Chris)

The woman moved with quiet strength. I kept watching her hands: the way she held the baby, poured the milk, wiped a child's face without breaking her stride. There was love in every gesture. When she hugged me, I felt something that surprised me: a kind of grief. A longing. Not just for a child, or a home, or even for Mongolia but for that kind of knowing, that rootedness. She belonged to this land in a way I've never belonged anywhere.

We couldn't speak the same language, but we made eye contact, smiled, and eventually embraced. I think we were the same age. She was so beautiful I couldn't stop staring at her. She might be the most beautiful woman I've ever seen. Strong, still, glowing. A quiet girl-crush. She even took a selfie of us together. I wished her the best of luck in life. I felt like I was part of their family even for just an hour.

We had to get back on the river not the road! Funny how I keep saying that. The river is our road now. We had a long day ahead and the heat had hit 36 degrees Celsius. The rapids were mostly gone only a few gentle grade ones remained. We stopped for lunch as a quick storm blew over. All eight of us huddled under a small tarp, so cosy! The storm was fun to watch, and I felt safe, squished in with my new friends. We had soup and bread, and as soon as it passed, the sun came blazing back.

When we arrived at camp, I was so impressed with Deb's progress. They're such a great team they never give up. Amazing. And Kev what a legend. So funny with his banter and Dad jokes. He keeps saying I have a 'lack of emotional intelligence' because I tease him about his age. I admit I do little digs on purpose, he picks up on them quick, so I do it more. His white powdered hair is too tempting not to joke about. But he laughs, I love him for it, and when I say he's like a Dad he's probably old enough to be my Grandad!

For an older guy, he's full of energy and stories. I can't wait to meet up with them in the UK. Deb is a delight - witty, quick, generous. And Kev talks openly about Afghanistan. I never hear those stories, and I know many people have been. It's rare for someone to share. I know what happened over there was horrific: the tours, the losses. So many young men never came home the same. Some didn't come home at all. He's been through a lot. He's got so much experience. I hope he writes a book. If he does, I'll be one of the first to buy it.

Chapter 13: Wild horses and river crossings

I woke up after a lovely night's sleep in my tent. I always sleep really well when I'm camping it's so nice to be close to the ground. Anyway, I made a schoolboy error. I'd left my shoes outside and didn't think anything of it, until I put my foot in one and quickly noticed something inside. I screamed loudly: something cold and wet had touched my toes. Slimy, but hard. My first thought was that I'd killed it. I pulled the shoe off, heart racing, and peeked in.

It was a toad. A massive toad in my shoe. I laughed so hard I fell on the floor giggling. The toad looked so settled, so content in there like he'd moved into a snug little flat. I managed to get a photo and gently encouraged him out without touching him, of course. You should never handle wild animals; the oil on your skin can harm them. He just hopped out like it was no big deal, and my shoes went back home. It could've been a snake. I guess I was lucky. And I guess the toad was lucky too he was still alive.

(Image: Rosemary)

The whole thing reminded me of when I was pregnant with my children. Animals used to show up around me all the time. I'd open the front door and there'd be a family of hedgehogs sitting right there. Stray dogs would wander into the house, cats meowing through the night outside my window. I don't know what it was, maybe animals can sense something in pregnant women. A softness. A safety. It made me think of my babies.

I gave birth to both of them textbook-style but with a strange twist. Twelve hours of labour each, but when they arrived, they were both born still inside their amniotic sacs. '*En caul*', I later learned it's called. It's meant to happen to one in a million babies and it happened to me twice. They told me it was rare, even unheard of. Painful too. Some cultures say that's a sign of extreme luck. Others say it's a curse. Either way, it was unforgettable. So are they. I miss them so much. Of course, they're teenagers now, probably loving the space. They always tell me I've got too much energy. Maybe this trip is a holiday for them as much as it is for me.

(Image: Chris)

We have reached our last river side campsite, and we are now all sad that our journey will be ending soon so we all have a big reflection laugh about the memories that we've made together and head to our tents. At night, in my little tent, I was woken by a strange sound thundering hooves, heavy breathing, the snorting of wild animals. At first, I thought I was dreaming. But then the sound grew louder, and louder, until it was all around me.

I held my breath. Twenty wild horses had surrounded my tent. Their hooves pounded the earth like drums. The noise was deafening, snorts and whinnies echoed across the dark. It was as if they were singing to each other, calling out through the night in a language I couldn't understand.

In the morning Kev said that he saw one leap straight over my tent. I must've just missed it, but I felt it, the rush of air, the tremble of the ground. I couldn't sleep after that. I lay there frozen, heart pounding, terrified one might trip and crush me in the dark. My thin canvas walls felt paper-thin, no match for a herd of galloping beasts.

But I was safe. Somehow, I was safe. And even through the fear, there was wonder. Being surrounded by wild horses in the middle of the Mongolian steppe, that's something I'll never forget. It felt like I'd stepped into another world, one where nature ruled completely, and I was just a visitor.

After packing up and loading the canoes, we set off again and stopped at another nomadic family's ger. We gave sweets and toys to the kids, who were really grateful. The river was calm. There were no accidents. Just smooth paddling.

Kev and Deb said they wanted to adopt me. If only they knew how much I would love that. I haven't said anything to them about my upbringing, but I hope they realise I'm taking that literally!

My canoe partner Davaaka said I'm like a sister to him. We have really bonded. He talked to me about his wife and children and said I'm a good woman, a good wife. He said I'm like a strong Mongolian woman. I was chuffed. Really chuffed. That meant more than I could say. I respect this culture so deeply, and to be told I belong in it that I've embraced it filled me with something deep and solid. Pride, maybe. Or peace. For the first time in a long time, I felt like I was exactly where I was meant to be.

As day nine dawned, we'd already covered over 300 kilometres. The mighty Delgermörön was behind us now, and we were approaching the confluence where it meets the Five Rivers. A Mongolian driver man told us we were the first English group to do this what an achievement. Me and Davaaka rushed ahead in our canoe, hearts pounding. We passed the sand dunes, the final stretch before the finish line.

I could hardly believe it. We waved to everyone else coming behind us. We've made it. We've done the river. I shouted it again, louder this time the words bursting out from somewhere deep inside me:

"We've done it! We've done it!"

Everyone climbed out of their boats, and hugs spread like wildfire. Some people cried, overcome by the sheer magnitude of what we'd achieved. I didn't cry, Nick did, but my heart was full so full it felt like it might burst.

Then, suddenly, Mark lifted me off the ground. I was surprised, maybe even a little stunned, I hadn't expected that from him. But I think he likes me now. And when he said in that deep voice of his that I was a 'very competent paddler', I was surprised to get a compliment.

The drivers were there waiting, waving at all of us, smiles wide and faces bright. The joy, that feeling, I can't put it into words. It was beyond joy. It was a moment of triumph, of transformation.

My body, my mind, my soul all changed by the river. I am a new person. I am Wilderness Rose. I have conquered rivers.

I have been in some of the wildest, most remote places on Earth places so far off the map no one can come to rescue you. I have touched lands that very few have ever reached. More people have stood on Everest than have completed this river. And now, I have too.

I stood there, breathless, listening to the rush of the river behind me, feeling the wind on my face, the earth firm beneath my feet. I closed my eyes for a moment and let it all wash over me the exhaustion, the pride, the disbelief. Then I shouted again, my voice carrying over the water:

"We've done it! We've made history!"

As night fell, my body felt tired but full of river water, wild stories, and the quiet pulse of belonging. I crawled into my tent, heart steady, and soon the songs of horses outside rocked me into sleep.

Chapter 14: Long road: 1000 kilometres to go

One Toyota Land Cruiser. One Russian UAZ. Eight tired paddlers and two drivers that didn't really understand us both language-wise and in temperament. We headed straight to the mountains. The terrain was sandy and bumpy and that's an understatement. Thank God I took my travel sickness pills with me.

(Image: Driver))

We drove for five hours and only covered 30 kilometres! Eventually, we found a perfect camping spot, surrounded by hills and an endless meadow. So peaceful and breathtaking. We all slept well.

We were up at 7am to load and start the porridge, and were out, fed, and packed by the roll call. Camping in the open after summer rain. The driver found the Russian van was playing up, so we had to drive to the nearest town to swap cars. Now we are in a Prius and Land Cruisers, a bit squashy, but manageable. We stopped at a service (Mongolian) for lunch near Lake Uvurkhangai, which was very interesting. The local infrastructure was basic, a code-in lock-house, with two women and teenagers helping in a shop. We had a long drop toilet that was incredibly smelly. We covered 350 kilometres that day and stayed at a camp in yurts. So cool!

It was the most modern yurt we'd come across with Wi-Fi and electricity, we're definitely starting to notice that we're coming out from the wild and into more civilised areas. It is happening slowly but we can see it very clearly after being in the wild for so long these little luxuries mean even more. At teatime, we all sat around a bowl, broke bread, and ate a Mongolian vegetable meal. Even the vegetable meal had meat, it's funny why they called it a vegetable meal when it was a meat meal.

Then they prepared a traditional Mongolian dish for us. We all went outside to watch them lay out the marmot at their version of a preparation area. It was unlike anything I've ever seen. They chopped off its head, pulled out all the insides, and filled the empty carcass with hot stones. Then they added the organs back in, packed in more stones, sewed it shut, plugged up the holes and finally, they used a flame torch to burn off all the hairs while it cooked from the inside.

I couldn't look away. It was disturbing yet mesmerising and completely normal to them. There was no drama or performance in it. Just tradition. I couldn't imagine this ever happening in the UK, and I knew instantly that this was one thing I was not going to eat. So I just hid behind the post quietly. I don't think anyone noticed. I mean, I've had the fermented horse milk. I've eaten everything they've given me the curd, the dry milk biscuits, but this? This I couldn't do. The nomadic farmer offered it out to everyone with such pride. His little daughter, she must've been about six, stood by his side beaming. Her hair had been shaved off, part of a special ceremony they do when a child reaches a certain age. She loved her Dad, the way she looked at him it was magical, she also loved the meat so got right in there.

Afterwards, we all went into the *gers*. We had a nightcap around 10pm, or 'jam o'clock' as Nick would say. We laughed, we chatted about the events of the day, then curled up to sleep, six of us per ger.

The next morning, we packed up again. That's when I noticed our new driver was a bit odd. He didn't quite drive like someone used to driving for a living. Turns out, he wasn't. They'd found him on a Facebook page after putting out a call: 'Anyone heading to Ulaanbaatar who can take a few travellers?' And this guy said yes. He wasn't a driver, just someone going the same direction.

Looking back, that explains a lot. His driving was terrible. But it's also kind of funny, in a way only Mongolia could deliver a complete stranger agreeing to take a car full of foreigners across some of the world's worst roads. He definitely got free food and places to stay out of it. I wonder if people do this back home? I mean, I would never. Stranger danger, right? But here? It just worked.

Anyone who's ever been to Mongolia would understand how bad the roads are. It's not just potholes, we're talking gaping holes in the pavements, missing kerbs, whole chunks of walkway just gone. Potholes have nothing on this place. At least back home they're in the roads, not where you're meant to walk!

After another day of relentless bumping and jostling, we had to change a tyre. Again. Another roadside tyre shop. They're everywhere here like corner shops back home. And no wonder, with the way these roads are. Tyres blow out all the time. The funny part? It only costs £1 to get it changed.

We stopped for the night at another guest house, another *ger*. That evening, we got to hang out with the locals again. They served us a lovely hot meal soup followed by horse milk for pudding. It was fizzy. Fizzy milk! Definitely an acquired taste. I never want to try it again.

The group was starting to feel it now tired, sore, travel-weary. Spirits were dipping. But me? I was still in 'positive vibes' mode.

"We've got this," I kept saying.

Davaaka and I had formed this unspoken connection. We could glance at each other and know exactly what the other was thinking. I want more food. What on earth are they doing?

It was hilarious. I'd bought some seaweed at a local shop and started eating it straight from the packet. Davaaka burst out laughing and took it out of my hands. "You don't eat seaweed like that," he said, still laughing hours later. Apparently, you're meant to cook it. Who knew? I thought it tasted fine. And hey, I didn't get sick, so it couldn't have been that bad.

After four long days of travelling, we finally reached our last destination: the city. But it still took us two hours to cover the final three kilometres in traffic. It was the worst traffic I've ever seen. If you're planning a visit, leave plenty of time for getting around. You can drive through the mountains faster than you can through the city.

We arrived at 3 pm, dumped our stuff, and decided to go to the famous Black Market. We took the bus, and the transition from wild, open countryside to crowded, chaotic market was surreal. Just days ago, we were surrounded by nomadic herders. Now? Thousands of people packed into a tin-roofed maze of stalls.

We were warned about pickpockets and drunk men. We didn't get robbed, just shouted at a few times. Kev, Chris, and Mark all bought traditional Mongolian coats. They really suited them. I hope they wear them back home. I'd like to see the looks they get on the high street.

The market was heaving when suddenly the skies opened. Rain, heavy and warm. I got excited and started dancing. The others joined in. Team Dad dancing. Singing. Splashing in puddles. The locals started filming us on their phones the crazy white people. But we didn't care. We were soaked through, laughing, totally in the moment. That moment bonded us again. What a team.

Back at the guest house, we got ready for our 'last supper'. We found a lovely Mongolian restaurant. Davaaka brought his wife and children to meet us his family, which was beautiful. His wife told us she hopes to have more children, so she can receive a medal from the government. They actually give medals for having four or more children, and again at six. It's part of a national effort to preserve traditional

Mongolian culture and increase the population. They want to protect the nomadic way of life.

We voted on group awards for the expedition:

- Paddler of the Week - Nick & Rose
- Most Improved Paddler of the Week - Nick
- Swimmer of the Week - Debs
- Fail of the Week - Kev
- Rescue of the Week - Davaaka (for the cow)
- Line of the Week - Debs
- Chef of the Week - Matt
- Guide of the Week - Davka
- Energiser Bunny Award - Rose
- Frog of the Week - Nick
- Happiest Person of the Week - Chris
- Photo of the Week - Mark

It was the perfect end, full of laughter, tears, and love. And then, it was over.

Postscript: July 2025

(Image: Nick)

The journey to the airport, the plane ride, the drive home all a blur. I walked through the front door and was instantly wrapped in hugs. My kids. My husband. Their faces lit up. But in that moment, I realised something else too: my two teenage children don't need me in the same way anymore. They're becoming independent. Me going away was good for them. And for me.

So if you're a Mum reading this, feeling guilty for leaving your children, don't. It's good for them to see you living your life. They learn from that. Even my husband had a good time while I was away. Okay, he didn't say he missed me, but I know he did.

After catching up on some much-needed sleep, it was time to face reality: unpack, wash the kit, scrub myself clean. I was filthy. My hair was so matted they'd nicknamed me "Yak Girl" in Mongolia. Simon tried his best to untangle it, but in the end, he had to cut the mats out. He kept the hair. Bit weird. But sweet. Told you he missed me.

I can't wait for the next adventure. Hopefully Simon comes with me next time. I told him this trip changed me. I see the world differently now. He replied:

> "I hope you haven't changed too much. I like who you are. You're the most amazing woman I've ever met."

A few days of catching up with emails, jobs, and then it was back to my usual rhythm: wake up, walk the dog, school run, work, gym, tea, bedtime. Sounds boring? It's not. Let me show you what a typical week looks like:

- Monday: Delivered a movement therapy session in a care home got everyone dancing, laughing. Pure joy. Then in the afternoon, another care home, another session this is where my oldest participant lives. She's 104. Still moving.

- Tuesday: Ran our intergenerational community group, followed by a dementia tea party, then another movement session. Ended the day with a Zoom call planning the next adventure with 12 women!

- Wednesday: Team-building day with college lecturers out on the river paddle boarding, jumping in, celebrating the end of term in the sunshine. Glorious.

- Thursday: One of my favourite care homes for more movement work, then taught a class at the local theatre.

- Friday: Delivered four sessions in a care school.

Not boring at all. I love what I do. I've made and created a life I love full of community, movement, connection. But Mongolia still echoes in me. That land of vast silence and big skies changed me.

After a childhood that offered more survival than safety, I now know who I am. I went to Mongolia in search of peace. And I found it where few would dare to go. Told through these raw diary entries, this memoir captures an extraordinary expedition down the Delgermörön River and the wildness both outside and within. From sofa-surfing teen to community leader and outdoor guide, this is my story.

It's a reminder that even the deepest scars can be softened by connection, culture, nature and the quiet determination to keep going. For anyone who's ever felt like they don't belong: you can find yourself. You can find your place. And it may be in the most unexpected place of all not just in the world, but within yourself.

And now here I am, at the end of this memoir, and I can't help but reflect on how far I've come. I think back to being off on my own at such a young age, fending for myself, sleeping on sofas and all the kind people I met along the way. In fact, ever since I left the home that never felt like a home, I haven't had anything but kindness and love from people.

Maybe it's because I chose to be that way. Or maybe I chose who I spent my time with, who I allowed in. Maybe it's all the skills I learned from the bad people I was raised by, and all the traumatic experiences I've faced.

Yes, I've seen evil. But I've also seen the best in people. And that gives me something: experience. You see, I was an angry girl once. I hated the world. I hated everyone. Right up into my mid-twenties, I carried that weight, a deep, burning feeling that I didn't belong anywhere, that nothing was safe, and no one was worth trusting. I was so angry with everything. And underneath the anger? Hurt. Abandonment. Silence.

But it was travelling that saved me. Culture. Connection. Adventure. Learning from people, from nature, from failure, from discomfort. Learning from my mistakes. Learning how to love. Learning how to trust. It took time. But I slowly became the woman I am today.

Now, I lead. I listen. I hold space. I know how to sit with discomfort. I know how to hold fear in one hand and courage in the other. I'm no longer just surviving I'm choosing. Choosing challenge. Choosing joy. Choosing to pass it on.

Maybe, just maybe, this book might help one person out there. If you've ever been through something really bad, and you've felt like no one understands, I hear you. To be fair, my experiences: no one does understand. I mean, how could they? Everyone's trauma is different. Everyone's story is different. You can't compare. It's not a game. Not who wins or loses. Not who had the worst time.

It's about coping. Accepting. Letting time do its work. Moving on. Letting go. I found my healing journey through adventure. Maybe it can be the same for you too.

There's something honest about challenging yourself, about facing the elements, about exploring, learning from different cultures, different people. About accepting that in life, bad things happen, but so do good things. And those good things are worth showing up for.

So thank you. For everything. To every place I've slept, every river I've crossed, every person who offered kindness, every version of myself I've been. And now: to you. The one reading this. This is the end of the book, but it's not the end of the journey.

Acknowledgments

My deepest thanks go to my dear husband, Simon. Your unwavering support, love, and belief in me made this journey possible. To my two amazing children, Roman and Marley, you are my greatest inspiration, my grounding force, and my wildest joy.

I am grateful to Clare, my brilliant editor, whose sharp eye and steady guidance brought clarity and strength to these pages, and to Kev, whose artistry brought this story to life on the cover, capturing its spirit with creativity and care.

To all my brothers and my beloved Granny, I carry your love with me always. To my incredible friends you know who you are your laughter, encouragement, and warmth have held me up more times than you'll ever know.

To everyone who has been part of this book, in ways both large and small, thank you.

To the Mongolia team: we shared something extraordinary, a bond forged in rivers, camps, and wild landscapes, a reminder that adventure is best when shared. To Matt, from Sweden Outdoor Coaching–this trip could not have happened without your steady leadership and commitment.

To my Mongolian brother, Davaaka paddling beside you was an honour. Your strength, humour, and heart brought depth to every moment of this journey.

And to the generous nomadic families and all the incredible Mongolian people we met along the way thank you for opening your homes, your hearts, and your world to us, leaving memories that will stay with me forever.

Appendix: Travel Preparations and Expedition Diary

Packing List and Expedition Kit

My packing was a mix of tested gear, thoughtful gifts, and a few last-minute lifesavers, all of which proved essential across beautiful Mongolian wilderness.

Favourite Kit Shout-Out:

- Gill dry bag: my most treasured piece of kit. It's been everywhere with me and never lets me down: without you, all my kit wouldn't be dry.

Food & Cooking:

- Jetboil stove with two gas canisters
- Boil-in-the-bag expedition meals
- Porridge sachets
- Flour for bread-making
- Packet soups
- Sweets and energy gels
- Hydration sachets
- Filtered water bottle, gifted by my two best friends, Sarah and Clare. A genuine lifesaver and timesaver!
- Millbank bags for additional water filtration

Navigation and Power:

- Physical map of the region (not ideal, but the best available)
- Offline digital maps downloaded to my phone (no signal, but still handy)
- Two Power Monkeys
- TPS Garmin and waterproof 2PS Garmin
- Compass all in an extra waterproof pouch

Fire and Survival:

- Rod and steel for fire-lighting
- Basic survival kit
- Superglue for emergency repairs
- Dry bags and extra dry pouches for keeping kit secure
- Nappy bags and wipes

First Aid and Health:

- Sun protection: Factor 50 sun cream
- Toothpaste & toothbrush
- Comprehensive first aid kit for head, stomach, feet
- Antibiotics (just in case)
- Antihistamines
- Black nasty tape (heavy-duty medical tape also good for fixing things)

Clothing:

- Three dry bags
- Ten pairs of socks (yes, ten)
- Ten pairs of pants
- Three clothing outfits
- A food stash for emergencies
- A Jetboil for heating water & ration packs
- Sleeping bag, warm coat, warm hat and gloves
- Two waterproof jackets and one pair of waterproof trousers
- Head torch and torch
- Diary and pen plus a spare pen
- Two fleeces
- Puncture repair kit for my dry bags and black and nasty tape, knife .
- Waterproof jacket, insulated jackets, T-shirts, vests, and long-sleeve tops – mostly from Mammut, who generously supported me through their community discount scheme: https://www.mammut.com/uk/en
- Shoes for the water that you're happy to walk on rocks & suitable for lining
- Good set of hiking boots
- Quick-dry technical clothing from ThruDark, who kindly sent me a few pieces I wore almost daily. Read more: https://www.thrudark.com/blogs/news/paddling-an-uncharted-river-in-mongolia

Journey Overview: Ulaanbaatar to the Five Rivers Confluence

Cultural Sites Visited:

- Chinggis Khaan National Museum – Opened 2022, expansive exhibits near Sukhbaatar Square
- Choijin Lama Temple Museum – Ornate 20th-century Buddhist temple and museum
- Gandantegchinlen Monastery – Ulaanbaatar's active monastery with giant Avalokiteśvara statue
- Genghis Khan Equestrian Statue – Iconic silver statue, 54 km east of Ulaanbaatar
- Erdene Zuu Monastery – Mongolia's oldest monastery, built on the ruins of ancient Karakorum

Pre-Expedition Travel:

- 2 nights in Ulaanbaatar then Traveled by road from Ulaanbaatar to the main airport (approx. 3 hours).
- Took a small, packed, and rather nerve-wracking plane to Mörön.
- Stayed overnight in a guesthouse in Mörön.
- The following day, drove for 5 hours over rough terrain from Mörön to the canoe launch site near the Russian border.

Canoe Expedition – Ulaan Taiga to the Five Rivers Confluence:

- Total paddled: Approx. 300 km (224 miles)
- River: Delgermörön, Northern Mongolia
- Start: High-altitude valleys near Belchir Uul in the Ulaan Taiga mountains, close to the Russian border
- Finish: Five Rivers Confluence near Tömörbulag, where the Delgermörön joins the Ider River to form the Selenga River
- Terrain: Remote wilderness with rugged canyons, open steppe, dense forest, and nomadic pastureland

Day-by-Day River Breakdown:

- Day 1: 22 km (13.7 miles) – River speed: 8–10 km/h. Rapids: Grade 2–3. Notable rapid: "Rosie Rapid"
- Day 2: 30 km (18.6 miles) – River speed: 6.7 km/h. Rapids: Grade 1–3. "Graveyard Rapid" with cave hazard on river right
- Day 3: ~33 km (20.5 miles) – Estimated speed: 7.5 km/h. Rapids: Mostly Grade 2, with one solid Grade 3
- Day 4: 42 km (26.1 miles) – River speed: 7.9 km/h. Rapids: Grade 1–2. Fast and friendly water
- Day 5: 60 km (37.3 miles) – River speed: 7.8 km/h. Rapids: Mostly Grade 1, with hidden strainers. Long, exposed day
- Day 6: 40 km (24.9 miles) – River speed: 7.5 km/h. Rapids: Grade 1, recurring strainers
- Day 7: 32 km (19.9 miles) – Estimated speed: 7.3 km/h. Rapids: Grade 1 with occasional strainers
- Day 8: 23 km (14.3 miles) – Estimated speed: 6.5–7 km/h. Rapids: Gentle Grade 1. Calm, steady water
- Day 9: 20 km (12.4 miles) – Estimated speed: 6.5 km/h. Mostly flatwater. Final push to confluence

On the river Campsites and Accommodation:

- Night 0: Guesthouse in Murun (Khovsgol Province)
- Night 1: Altraga launch site, Bayanzurkh Village
- Night 2: "Graveyard" campsite
- Night 3: mountains like dinosaurs campsite (lots of rain)
- Night 4: flat ground campsite (the long portages)
- Night 5: Tultiin Tokhoi Camp
- Night 6: Wide river – Wild camp
- Night 7: The Island of Horns campsite
- Night 8: Hot wild swim campsite
- Night 9: Wild camp
- Night 10: Tömörbulag (mountain views, near the confluence)
- Night 11: Guesthouse, Tariat (near Khorgo Crater)
- Night 12: Guesthouse, Kharkhorin (former Mongol capital)
- Night 13: Guesthouse, Ulaanbaatar (final night)

Post-Expedition Travel:

- After reaching the Five Rivers Confluence, we travelled over 1,000 km (approx. 620 miles) back to Ulaanbaatar by motor vehicles.
- The drive crossed mountains, rocky roads, and endless potholes, a bumpy, exhausting, and unforgettable return.

Villages, Valleys & Roadside Stops:

- Tumurbulag – Five Rivers confluence area; site of the infamous "seaweed mistake"
- Jargalant – Vehicle swap point
- Tsakhir (Avgaldai) – Remote, peaceful mountain valley
- Tariat & Khorgo Crater – Volcanic landscapes, mountain ravioli, and marmot dinner
- Tsetserleg – Lively town with a meat feast and supply chaos
- Ikh Tamir – Tyre rescue stop
- Khotont – Sampling fermented mare's milk (airag)
- Kharkhorin – Stroll through Mongolia's historic former capital
- Elsen Tasarkhai – Stretch of sand dunes and semi-desert
- Lun – Return to more populated areas
- Burentogtokh – Final lunch stop before paddling
- Ulaanbaatar – Journey's end

Top Tips from the River

These are things I've learned the hard way through trial, error, discomfort, and plenty of mud over the years. None of it came from a guidebook, just experience earned one cold toe or soggy sock at a time.

- Period pants are a game changer. Comfortable, no-fuss, and easy to manage on expeditions.
- Quick-dry socks. Trust me, pack extra. Dry feet keep your spirits up.
- Spend money on a proper sleeping bag and down jacket. The right ones will last a lifetime and keep you safe.
- Always have a dry bag in a dry bag in a dry bag. Even my amazing Gill bag (a ride-or-die companion) isn't immune to bad luck. Layer up you won't regret it.
- Take knee pads for canoeing. Your knees will thank you after 6+ hours a day.
- Roll mats are tiny these days take two! Double up for insulation and comfort without using extra space. Worth it for the queen-level sleep.
- Merino wool socks under neoprene socks on cold days. Warmth, breathability, and comfort in one.
- Wipes are a game changer in the wild as long as you've got nappy bags to carry them out until you find a proper bin. Otherwise, moss is a decent backup!
- Moss can also be used for washing. It has natural antibacterial properties, good for face, hands, and even scrubbing pans, yep, really.
- Don't sleep in all your layers. Your sleeping bag needs body heat to work properly. Use coats and thick jackets on top like an extra blanket instead.
- Always travel with a waterproof phone case. Whether for navigation or capturing memories, keep it protected.

I've got plenty more, but those will have to wait for the next book...

If you want to explore more photographs and stories about Mongolia, use the QR code for Rosemary's digital gallery on her website, or use this link to go to https://www.wyeknotcommunity.com/

@WYE_KNOT_COMMUNITY